MORE PICTURES OF RAINHAM

These are two of the earliest pictures I have seen of Rainham. The 1834 print of St Margaret's Church is clearly recognisable although many details have changed. The wooden building by the Churchyard wall is the 'Lockup' or prison — one wonders how often it was put to use! The most notable absence from this picture is the row of chestnut trees so obvious in every other view I have ever seen of the Church. The five trees we know today were reputedly planted by the landlord of the White Horse (Mr Sayer) during the last years of the old century to commemorate the birth of his children. At this time Rainham parish was in the rural deanery of Sittingbourne, the Archdeaconry of Maidstone and the Diocese of Canterbury. The living had been given in 1136 together with a number of others to found Leeds Abbey, near Maidstone, by Robert de Crevecoeur. When the monasteries were dissolved by Henry VIII the living reverted to the crown and was eventually presented to the Archbishop of Canterbury in whose gift it remained until 1928 when Rainham became part of Gillingham Borough and subsequently Rochester Diocese, a change few remember now but which caused much ill feeling at the time as Rainhamites had no wish to become submerged in the conglomeration of Gillingham. The parish has been an inhabited place from ancient times, formerly being known as 'Renham'. Evidence of Roman occupation may still be found at Otterham Quay in the shape of pottery fragments and implements embedded in the silt. The Tufton family, Earls of Thanet and ancestors of Lord Hothfield who was a landowner at the turn of the century, have a long association with Rainham. The Tufton Chapel in the Church contains a number of fine tombs and monuments to the family, many of whom lie buried in the vaults below. Some were transferred from Hothfield Church whose vaults were often flooded.

An unusual view of Rainham sometime between the coming of gas to the street (1870) and the arrival of the trams (1906). The cart was probably parked while the horse was being reshod at the forge.

GAS COMES TO RAINHAM

In the latter half of the 19th century Rainham began to make changes which started its evolution to the prosperous town it has now become. One great change was the introduction of gas for heating and lighting which made it possible to hold church services and club meetings in the winter evenings. The Parish Magazines of 1868 tell of the struggle to raise the necessary funds to install gas in the church "so that the present generation and their successors will reap the benefit of it in the increased warmth and dryness of their church as well as the improvement in light and the diminished cost of gas as against candles."

"The 24th February 1868 will be remembered as the day on which gas lighting was first introduced to Rainham Street. An illuminated star was exhibited at the White Horse in honour of the event, but the wind somewhat interfered with the success of the experiment. The unusual sight, however, afforded great pleasure to a considerable number of lookers-on, and the effect of the light on the fine tower of the church was particularly striking. Now that gas is obtainable, it will be for the parishioners to decide whether the darkness of the street shall be enlightened and the church be at once warmed and illuminated."

It obviously was so decided as by January 1870 Rainham Street was lit from Mr G. Green's (just west of Orchard Street) to Drury Lane (High Dewar Road) and Station Road down to the station. The lamp lighter was Henry Honey and he entered his duties for the first time on Christmas Eve 1869.

A Vestry meeting at this time decided to raise money by subscription to provide gas burners and stoves in the church. By the end of January £34 6s 6d had been raised and on February 21st it was resolved to accept the tender of Messrs Taylor and Son for £58 15s to complete the work. This enabled the church to be lit for the first time on Palm Sunday April 10th when a special evening service was held at seven o'clock. Mr Taylor's bill was finally paid off in August 1873.

A curious entry in the magazine of 1873: "The retiring inspectors were re-elected and the usual application made to the overseers for £29, the cost of lighting the street." Does this mean that the parish as a whole bore the cost of lighting the two lamps at the church steps?

MR GEORGE GREEN

Mr George Green who died in 1913 at the age of 87 years owned this shop for many years and carried out his carpentry and undertaking businesses from these premises. He was a remarkable man and well respected in Rainham. He came as a young man of 19 on a visit to his sister Mrs Henty, whose husband was schoolmaster of Upchurch, from Warwick and remained in Rainham for the rest of his life. He worked for Mr J. Taylor, carpenter – builder, and married a daughter of his employer. He had two sons and two daughters. Mr Green was a very skilled joiner and turner and went into business on his own account as a builder and undertaker, his sons joining him when they grew up. Mr Green's skills were numerous and he made his own tools for his trade. In his early days Rainham Church clock had only an hour hand but Mr Green cleverly put in a minute hand which was still in use after his death. He also made the wooden steps and hand rails which may be seen in many pictures of the old Cricketers public house. Mr Green was a man of many talents being a master of Astronomy, Euclid and Algebra and was a keen student of electricity. He was said to have a photographic memory but with all his profound knowledge he was extremely reticent and modest and it was only when conversing with a kindred spirit that he could be drawn out on any of these subjects. Mr Green was also a great authority on bee-keeping and won several medals in competition for bee-keeping appliances, one of which, known as the Rainham Hive, became famous.

Before the advent of the County Police, Mr Green served as the village constable, and being a man of over 6 foot and of good physique he was a personage to be respected. Before the days of the railway Mr Green thought nothing of walking to Gravesend to get a train to London and completing the return walk that same night. A kindly man, it is related of him that whilst he was a young man a gipsy died in his tent at Meresborough from smallpox. Mr Green carried out his undertaking duties and was paid by the widow of the gipsy all in threepenny pieces.

Mrs Nicholson took over the shop after Mr Green's death and was helped by her daughter when she became old enough. As may be seen from the photographs they sold tobacco and sweets and were well known as the local agents for the Maidstone and District Bus Co. Miss Nicholson hand wrote the display boards advertising the cost of travel by coach for over forty years. In the 1930s it cost 8/- return to Brighton, 4/- to Margate and 3/6d to Sheerness. Seats could be booked at the Nicholsons' shop and the appropriate coach boarded nearby. Just prior to the war the shop was given a new front which may be seen in the 1937 photograph decorated in honour of the Coronation of George VI. Miss Nicholson was forced by ill health to retire in the late 1960s and the building is now part of Lloyds Bank.

The weatherboarded cottages long since demolished were then the homes of Mr Holloway the lamp lighter and Mr Chambers.

The history of Rainham National School was fairly well documented in the Picture Book of Old Rainham. The earlier of these two pictures shows it before the front steps were built. Former pupils will remember the tap at the foot of the chimney and perhaps recollect that it was turned by means of a key which was held by the caretaker, Mr F. Ockwell. In very hot weather he would leave a bucket of water on the stone base and hands clean or dirty were used for drinks.

The Infants School of 1906/7 with their teacher Mrs Brice (back row extreme left). Amongst the children are R. Chambers, H. Bennett, A. Plum, H. Wickens, H. Nicholls, W. Samson, H. Kemp, V. Marser and Howland.

RAINHAM NATIONAL SCHOOLS

The original National School building was erected in 1846 and the plaque in the wall of the chimney gives credit to the Earl of Thanet who donated the site. This stone was carefully removed when the building was demolished in 1977 and may now be seen in St Margaret's Junior School, Orchard Street.

By 1866 the school was inadequate for the number of children attending and the single storey Infants School was added at a cost to the parishioners of £507.

An entry in the Parish Magazine for May 1868 states "The new Infant School with an additional classroom is now finished. It is built in a very substantial manner and must, it is thought, give satisfaction to the inhabitants in general. As the Government will not pay the amount of their grant (£40) until all the other subscriptions have been received, it is hoped that those connected with the parish by residence or property, who have not yet assisted in this good work, will at once come forward and wipe out the deficiency which prevents the opening of the room. Any sum however small will be thankfully received."

January 1869

"The committee in laying the above balance sheet before their friends beg to congratulate them on the completion and opening of the new Infant Room of which the good effect is already visible. The Parishioners are informed that Infants from the age of 2½ years are now admitted to the school."

However the 'substantially built' new room was to suffer a sad fate for in January 1875 just six years after opening we read, "A sad accident occurred at the National School on Wednesday December 9th. About 1.15 pm a portion of the South end of the building gave way, and fell upon some children who were playing beneath it. Of the six children who were more or less injured F. Longley, J. Grant, J. Tadman, A. Frid, Albert Gulvin and A. Rayner all have since done well, though it was feared at one time that the first at any rate had sustained injuries which would terminate fatally."

On Sunday December 20th collections for the relief of the injured were made in the Parish Church amounting to £6 16s 0d and in the Congregational and Ivy Street Chapels – amounting to £1 6s 8½d. At a meeting held at the Institute on Thursday 7th January 1875 it was resolved (Mr Longley (headmaster of the school) having declined to receive any benefit from the fund) that the sum of £8 2s 8½d collected on behalf of the children injured in the accident at the school be distributed in the following manner:

	£	s	d
Mr Everest bill		18	6
Dr Penfold bill	2	18	2½
Mrs Sayers bill		6	0
J. Grant	1	0	0
J. Tadman	1	0	0
A. Frid	1	0	0
J. Gulvin		10	0
A. Rayner		10	0
	£8	2	8½

Up to the end of the 1914-18 war children were encouraged to attend school regularly by the offer of medals for a perfect year and a certificate if only up to 8 sessions were missed. (A school day then as now was counted as 2 sessions.) In 1908 the possible attendances were 421 — presumably only half days were worked on breaking up day. Some conscientious, and healthy, pupils even managed to obtain bars to their original medal for a further year's perfect attendance. The rewards were distributed at the Empire Day Celebrations and being great treasures many of them have survived. The examples above belong to my uncle, Frank Thomas.

The National School at the top of Station Road as it will be remembered by many — the appearance barely changed until its demolition in 1977 to make way for the Rainham Shopping Precinct. In 1908 at about the time of this photograph the school had accommodation for 600 children but no departments were in fact full — the number on roll being 200 boys, 150 girls and 190 infants; total 540. The teaching staff were as follows:

Boys Department: Messrs Samuel Hodson (Headmaster), G.R. Bone and V. Way, the Misses R.E. Campbell and G. Campbell and Messrs S.A. Hodson and E.V. Pierce.

Girls Department: Mrs Charlesworth (Head Mistress), Miss Holman, Mrs Richards, Mrs Woollett, Miss Rickells and Miss G. Taylor.

Infants Department: Mrs A. Brice (Head Mistress), Miss Smith, Miss Gooding, Miss Bolton and Miss Ratcliffe.

LOWER RAINHAM SCHOOL

It is unfortunate that we have not been able to find a picture of this building which has been replaced by a new house. A word or two of its history might interest some of our readers. By 1876 the National School at the top of Station Road was becoming decidedly overcrowded, many of the children having to walk long distances (four times a day) from Meresborough, Rainham Mark and Lower Rainham. It was therefore decided to put off enlarging the school in favour of building at Lower Rainham. Half a piece of land was given by Sir Henry Tufton's estate opposite the Ancient Mariners public house and a single roomed school erected and opened by the end of 1875. An extract from the Parish Magazine December 1876 reads "The schoolroom at Lower Rainham was nicely decorated and a satisfactorily attended service held in it on Christmas evening." Previously Bible classes had been held in Bloors Place superintended by a daughter of the house, Miss Maria Smart. Similar meetings were held at Meresborough. In August 1874 it had been resolved to open a subscription for defraying the cost (£250) of the new school required at Lower Rainham. Mr Seager's tender (the lowest) was for £189 but of course a considerable sum was required for fittings, bringing the total cost to £250.

The school room was first used for a Harvest Festival Service in 1875 and on October 11th the school opened with 51 infants under the school mistress Mrs Wallis. Children from the age of 2½ years were eligible to attend. School attendance at that time was still voluntary. Later children up to 9 years were taught. The school continued doing good work until the building of the Senior Schools in Orchard Street in 1932 left room in the National and Council Schools for the children of Lower Rainham. Consequently the school was closed and the children travelled by bus to their new schools. The building at Lower Rainham was in use as a Church Room until the war, then it stood forlorn and empty for a few more years but is now only a memory.

KENT MESSENGER PHOTOGRAPH OF THE CHURCH OF ENGLAND GIRLS' SCHOOL RAINHAM 1925
Headmistress Miss A.R. Osborn

Back Row: N. Farrell, G. Gooding, O. Filmer, V. Chaplin, M. Baker, W. Hearnden, C. Filmer, R. Benham, K. Cheal, W. Dumbrell, R. Allen, F. Hodges, V. Castle, J. Palmer.

Second Row: H. Thompson, E. Barett, M. Kitney, K. Andrews, K. Holdstock, P. Norris, E. Tayler, B. Chapman, E. Strood, E. Naylor, D. Smith, M. Packham, R. Major, H. Phillips, E. Smith.

Third Row: G. Gannon, M. Parsons, E. Godden, E. Barrett, H. Shepherd, E. Ratcliffe, F. Cox, M. Kent, J. Upton, T. Martin, K. Bingham, M Culmer, E. Stringer, N. Smith, M. Chapman, E. Bond.

Front Row: I. Strood, F. Ward, M. Swan, I. Harvey, B. Deed, K. Howting, I. Hammond, E. Wickenden.

KENT MESSENGER PHOTOGRAPH OF THE CHURCH OF ENGLAND BOYS' SCHOOL RAINHAM 1925
Headmaster Mr G.R. Bone

Back Row: F. Sutton, R. Black, G. Bennett, A. Chaplin, C. Hempstead, N. Norris, W. Culmer, B. Hales, F. Andrews, H. Hammond, G. Thompson, W. Reed, D. Oldland, R. Godden, J. Hopkins, F. Tyler, E. Garlinge, W. Hodge.

Second Row: H. Thomas, S. Wheeler, A. Goodin, G. Packham, P. Holdstock, P. Brooker, F. Wickens, A. Allen, S. Smith, R. Collins, J. Hall, P. Charters, T. Wheeler, A. Newnham, A. Glanville, L. Hadaway, R. Brooks.

Third Row: F. Hadaway, D. Wickens, F. Cheal, W. Jarvis, R. Holme, W. Sayer, G. Horn, H. Gowers, Miss G. Campbell, Mr G.R. Bone, Mr S. Blackman, Miss D. Rodwell, E. Deed, E. Buck, T. Filmer, E. Benham, J. Sinclair, J. Smith, T. Stacey, E. Wickenden, Potter.

Fourth Row: P. Morris, H. Wickenden, J. Sawkins, A. Burr, W. Holmes, H. Parsons, A. Gowers, F. Strevens, W. Gowers, G. Oldland, A. Hales, R. Philpott, L. Partridge, S. Cross, F. Shepherd, M. Smith, L. Tong, A. Naylor.

Front Row: F. Briggs, E. Oliver, R. Jemmett, F. Horn, W. Gillman, P. Ward, E. Oliver, St. G. Hiscock, E. Stacey, S. Blundy, E. Wickenden, L. Brown, D. Packham, P. Cooper, A. Phillips, J. Coppins, S. Stroud, S. Filmer, H. Reed, T. Penfold, H. Howting, L. Oldland, R. Green, H. Harden, P. Trice, W. Blundy.

A boys' class at the National School c.1928.

THE SCHOOL TREAT

For years the Day School Treat followed a pattern no doubt eagerly anticipated in 1875 but which I fear would not come up to the expectations of modern youth.

"The school treat took place on Wednesday August 11th, a bright and warm day. At two o'clock the children proceeded to Church where after a short service performed by the Vicar they were addressed by the Rev. J.P. Alcock of Ashford who, after referring to the death of two of their companions (one of whom was to be buried that afternoon) spoke to them on the sin of using bad words. From the Church a procession, headed by the Infants, was formed to Berengrave, and here on the lawn they were entertained with cake, wine, milk etc to their hearts content. Returning to the meadow at the back of the school, kindly lent by Mr Prentis, they were again regaled with cake and tea. The usual games (cricket, kiss in the ring, and racing for prizes) followed, until the 'shades of the evening' compelled all to seek their homes, tired but happy."

The Old Folks' Tea took place on the same day at 6 o'clock. Widows and others receiving parochial relief sat down to a substantial repast of beef, mutton, ham, vegetables, cakes, bread and butter and tea.

A Junior School class from the 1930s
Back row from the left: Stan Jarvis, Fisher, Lew Collins, Tommy O'Brien, Peter Flynn.
Middle row: girl, Leslie Eccles, C. Still, Kenneth Stanley, boy, girl.
Front row includes: Pat Turner, Beryl Brenchley, Betty Adie, Joan Fullager.

NIGHT SCHOOL

The Vicar and his assistants held a Night School which in 1870 met on forty nights for more than 1½ hours on each occasion. There were 53 names on the books, the average attendance being about 30. Instruction was given in reading, writing, arithmetic and dictation, after which a chapter of scripture was read by the Vicar. According to custom those who attended 24 or more times were entertained at a supper held in the school rooms on April 27th.

A mixed Junior class from the 1950s whilst G.K. Turner was Headmaster.

In these aerial views of the old Church School it can be seen how little space was then considered necessary for playground. Latterly the boys did rather better than the girls as they were taken by Mr Turner to play football on the recreation ground. At the back of the school a small portion of the adjoining field was hired for the boys' garden plots. A small portion of the playground was sold to Barclays when the bank was built. It was then not possible to watch funerals at the church from the playground – this had traditionally been a playtime bonus.

These pictures taken in 1977 bring to an end the history of the old Church School building. Some people thought the historic building should have been preserved. It had however (under the constant threat of imminent demolition) been allowed to deteriorate since the schools left to move to their new homes in Orchard Street 10 years earlier and would have been very costly to repair and maintain. It occupied a prime site in the town and one has to admit the new shopping precinct has brought a much needed asset to Rainham.

RAINHAM C.E. SCHOOL

1846-1953

Reunion of Teachers and Scholars held on Saturday, 16th May, 1953 (Coronation Year).

ST MARGARET'S SCHOOLS

In 1932, following the Education Acts demanding secondary education for all, the Orchard Street Secondary Modern Schools were built. (See page 10 for a picture of the official opening.) Thirty years later Rainham had grown to such an extent that many more school places were needed. Two brand new secondary schools were built for senior pupils as Rainham School for Girls and the Howard School for Boys and so the redundant Orchard Street buildings were able to undergo a thorough facelift and conversion. The old Boys' School became the St Margaret's C of E Junior School, and the former Girls' School adapted to the St Margaret's Infants School. This aerial photograph was taken soon after extra buildings had been added in the quad area but before the new Dining Hall and Canteen were built adjoining the rear of the Infant School. For some years the schools were full to capacity and overflowing into the huts which had to be used as classrooms, however the building of new schools at Thamesview and particularly Mierscourt relieved the congestion and the two schools took on more manageable proportions, nicely fitting their accommodation with a little breathing room to spare. The building of an integral dining area released the huts in the foreground of the picture which are now used by the Marlborough Unit.

In 1977 the Infants School with their Headmistress Mrs J. Coates celebrated the Silver Jubilee of Queen Elizabeth II with a march from school along Thames Avenue, up Maidstone Road and back to Orchard Street via Broadview Avenue. It was led by a Scottish piper, Mr Jimmy Miller.

The staff of St Margaret's Junior School 1986. Mr Straaten has been Headmaster since 1964 and will be remembered by many past pupils. Several members of the staff have equal years of long service to the school. Back row from the left: Mrs Wilkes, Mrs Hunt, Mr Bellars, Mrs Relf, Mrs Ghosal, Mrs Pidduck, Miss Currell.
Front row: Mrs Fender, Mrs Tombs, Mr Smith, Mr Straaten, Mrs Chalmers, Mrs Wootten, Miss Jay.

The official opening of the Rainham Secondary Schools was on January 18th 1933. This photograph shows the Marquis of Dufferin and Ava opening the door, having been handed the key by the architect.

A cookery lesson in progress in 1937. This room is now Infant Class 6.

The wartime staff of Rainham Secondary Girls School.

Pupils and staff from the Rainham Secondary Schools walking down Orchard Street in September 1939 on their way to the station to catch a train which would take them to their new wartime home for the duration of the evacuation.

A form group taken in the quad at Rainham Senior Girls School c.1953.

Back row: Eva Gerard, Marion Smith, Pat Cheeseman, Christine Hales, Ann Jacobs, Taloula McCalister, Ellen Gilbert, Marcia Alexander, Janet Ransley, Kay Dumbrell, Joan Back.

Third row: Pauline Willis, Margaret Brown, Pat Wood, June Broad, Sheila Smith, Janet Brooker, Jean Caruthers, Shirley Crombell, Brenda Market, Janice Tassel, Valerie North.

Second row: Valerie Crockford, June Punyer, Dorothy Pateamny, Jean Spier, Wendy Barnes, Ann Wickenden, Valerie Syfleet, Dorothy Baylis, Wendy Bushel, Olive Harris.

Front row: Catherine Humphreys, Joyce Edy, Gill Benham, Jane Pym, Ann Clacket, Jean Campbell, Janet Payne.

RAINHAM SECONDARY SCHOOLS

During the 55 years of Rainham Senior Girls' School (now Rainham School for Girls) history there have been only three head teachers. Miss Hare was appointed to the position in 1932 and continued for many years after her marriage to Mr Smith, the Headmaster of the adjoining Boys' School. Miss Saunders became Headmistress in September 1964, leaving in 1979, and the present Headmistress, Mrs Snape, took up her duties in September 1980. For the first 36 years the school was in the Orchard Street building, but in 1968 moved to its present splendid site adjacent to the A2 sharing a large campus with Howard Secondary/Grammar School for Boys. Rainham now considers itself very fortunate to have such excellent schools within its boundaries.

A winning team on the same field, with the grass in rather better condition, collecting their cup on Sports Day in the 1950s.

Physical Education in the 1940s. Probably in preparation for the 1945 Victory Fete held at Berengrave (see page 23). This practice is taking place on the field behind the Orchard Street Schools. It reminds me of my own school uniform list of 1956 when our navy knickers were required to have elastic at the waist and knees.

By the 1970s in their modern building sport had taken on a whole new meaning for many Rainham girls. Volleyball and Badminton are being played here in the Sports Hall under the watchful eye of Miss Lucas.

Rainham School for Girls, opened in 1968.

The Library, Rainham School for Girls.

Rainham Secondary Boys' School — Form 1A, 1934
Back row from left: Golding, Pantony, Wilkins, Chantler, Gransden, Naylor, Mannington, Morley, Williams, Wood, Neat.
Second row: Clout, Whitehead, Eccles, Trafford, Tutt, ?, Miles, Bridge, Thompson.
Third row: ?, Springate, Humphries, Morris, Quinn, Gill, Swan, ?, Bigg, ?, ?.
Front row: Goodhew, Hatton, ?, ?, Gooding, McLeod, Gilbert, Smith.
The master is Mr Ingham.

RAINHAM COUNCIL SCHOOLS

By the beginning of this century the population of Rainham had risen to 4,800 and the National Schools could no longer accommodate the rising generations. Additional classes were held in the Orchard Street and Wakeley Road Chapels until a new Council School was built at the end of the unmade and usually very muddy Solomon Road. From the 1908 Directory we read: "These schools were erected in 1906 at a cost of £4,500. The buildings are a perfect type of a modern scholastic establishment and comprise a large assembly hall surrounded by classrooms."

Built to accommodate 250 children it was immediately enlarged to take 400. The hall became an asset to Rainham and concerts, socials and political meetings enjoyed a new venue.

Rainham Council Schools.

OPENING CEREMONY

SIX P.M.,

Wednesday, May 1st, 1907.

PERCY WAKELEY, ESQ.,

CHAIRMAN OF MANAGERS, WILL PRESIDE.

OPENING HYMN.

ALL people that on earth do dwell,
Sing to the Lord with cheerful voice;
Him serve with fear, His praise forth tell,
Come ye before Him, and rejoice.

The Lord, ye know, is God indeed;
Without our aid He did us make;
We are His flock, He doth us feed,
And for His sheep He doth us take.

O enter then His gates with praise,
Approach with joy His courts unto;
Praise, laud, and bless His name always,
For it is seemly so to do.

For why? the Lord our God is good;
His mercy is for ever sure;
His truth at all times firmly stood,
And shall from age to age endure.

To Father, Son, and Holy Ghost,
The God whom Heav'n and earth adore,
From men and from the Angel-host
Be praise and glory evermore. Amen.

DEDICATORY PRAYER.

OPENING OF BUILDING

BY

F. S. W. CORNWALLIS, ESQ.,

VICE-CHAIRMAN OF THE KENT COUNTY COUNCIL,

TO BE FOLLOWED BY

DISTRIBUTION OF MEDALS AND CERTIFICATES TO THE SCHOLARS.

The following Gentlemen have promised to be present:—

DR. T. B. NAPIER, M.P.
F. WINCENT, Esq., Vice-Chairman of the Kent Education Committee.
F. W. CROOK, Esq., B.A., Secretary, Kent Education Committee.
CHOL. HARRISON, Esq., M.A., Assistant-Secretary, Kent Education Committee.
R. G. E. LOCKE, Esq., C.C.
DR. PENFOLD, Chairman of the Rainham Parish Council.
G. E. BOND, Esq., Architect of the School.
W. L. GRANT, Esq.

CLOSING PRAYER.

NATIONAL ANTHEM.

GOD save our gracious King,
Long live our noble King,
God save the King.
Send him victorious,
Happy and glorious,
Long to reign over us,
God save our King.

O Lord, our God, arise,
Scatter his enemies,
And make them fall.
Confound their politics,
Frustrate their knavish tricks,
On Thee our hopes we fix.
God save us all.

Thy choicest gifts in store,
On him be pleased to pour,
Long may he reign.
May he defend our laws,
And ever give us cause
To sing with heart and voice,
God save the King.

Printed at the East Kent Gazette Office, Sittingbourne.

Until 1932 the school taught children from 5 to 14 years having mixed classes except for the top boys and girls. Cookery and Woodwork were still taught in the Station Road Methodist Chapel School room.

When Gillingham Council incorporated Rainham new schools were built in an extended Orchard Street (see preceding pages) and children of 11 and over were removed from the badly overcrowded Council School. This then became an Infant and Junior school only. One teacher from this period remembers teaching 70 Infants in a room which displayed a printed notice stating the room was designed to take 48 children. After the exodus of the seniors the hall could once more be used for the purpose intended: for too long it had been an additional classroom.

Rainham Council School

REUNION DINNER

in the Co-operative Hall, Rainham
on Saturday, 17th October, 1953
at 6.30 p.m.

Toasts

The Queen
Proposed by E. M. Clark, Esq.

Our Guest
Proposed by E. M. Clark, Esq.
Response by Mrs. M. F. Seago
Chairman: Mrs. W. Dartnall

After Dinner Entertainment

SOCIAL

Dancing to Electra Radio
M.C. R. Webb, Esq.

Light Refreshments during Evening

By 1950 the Council School was again full to overcrowding and a new Wakeley Road Junior School was built to take the children over 7 years of age. Now called Meredale Infants School the building still stands as a tribute to the enlightened days at the turn of the century. Two permanent relics remain to remind the children of their school's proud history; the bell which hung in the turret for so many years calling the children to school may still be seen, likewise the War Memorial plaque of the 1914-18 war is in the hall.

Council School Class 10, 1931. The other half of this Infant Class in Room 3 appears on page 20 of 'A Picture Book of Old Rainham'.

Standard Five, Council School, 1931
Mr Smart, Teacher

Standing row: L. Hyland, J. Lamb, ?, Mr Smith, Mr Smart, ?, ?, D. Riddle, A. Lavender, J. Kitchingham, E. Costin, R. Naylor, V. Best, D. Hitchcock, E. Hopper, E. Lacey, J. Golding, M. Renolds.
Fourth row: B. O'Connell, R. Pointer, ?, M. Wildish, ?, D. Allsop.
Third row: J. Davis, ?, D. Tutt, P. Ridley, P. Thomsett, F. Gifford, E. Hughes, K. Smith.
Second row: ?, R. Hinds, T. Pilkington, T. Parnell, A. Cook, D. Hughes, ?, Iris Baker.
First row: Hales, B. Godwin, P. Springate, Webb, K. Blake, E. Gooding, W. Collins, B. Barden.
Just off photo: Helen Stringer, E. Smitherman.

Reunion Dinners of the Rainham Council school were held as an annual event in the 1950s. Some of those present at the 1953 dinner were (from the back left): Mrs Major, Mr and Mrs Whitehead, E. Blundy, Mr and Mrs Rogers, Mr and Mrs Dartnell, Miss Springate, Miss Seago, Mr and Mrs Clark, W. Jordan, Mr and Mrs Samson, Mr and Mrs Golding, Mrs Long, Mrs Robinson, Mr and Mrs Brenton, Miss Blundy, Mrs Gooding, Mrs Mudge, Mrs R. Chambers.

ST MARGARET'S CHURCH

The Parish Church of Rainham is dedicated to St Margaret and is a large imposing building dating from the Early English period but with later additions. The large tower was much damaged by a violent storm on October 20th 1791. The fine east window was erected at a cost of £150, contributed by parishioners as a memorial to the Diamond Jubilee of Queen Victoria. The window was placed in position in January 1898. In June 1898 Mr Daniel Wills of Garfield House, Park Road, Sittingbourne presented to the parish three-quarters of an acre of land adjoining the Churchyard for the purpose of increasing the burying space. A brass tablet was erected in the south aisle commemorating the event. In 1985 a further portion of land was given to the Church, but as yet its use is undecided.

On January 20th 1869 the following letter was received by the Vicar and Churchwardens from the Canterbury Diocesan Architect:

"Dear Sirs,

This fine Church, dedicated to St Margaret, needs complete restoration . . . The Perpendicular tower no doubt was formerly a beacon

connected with a line of other churches from the coast to London. The fabric has suffered much from time decay and former repairs. The Chancel I found had not been touched — and in addition to the floor being carefully relaid, with the original levels made good, proper stall seats are required; the present unsightly framing at the east end should be removed and if practicable a simple reredos erected in its place. The walls are in a fair state but some repairs are needed.

In the body of the church the windows have almost entirely perished and require to be very carefully renewed or restored with the inner arches, jambs, cills etc made good. The modern dormer openings on the south side of the nave roof are no longer needed, they should be removed and the openings filled up. Seats for children are required and space for such could be fixed in the tower to accommodate about 70 children. The west doorway and door ought to be renewed."

The letter explains that the fabric in the N.W. respond is in a serious and dangerous condition from previous alterations and should not be neglected. It continues:

"The north porch facing the street is modern — very incongruous and in a bad state of decay — it should be rebuilt — the south porch also needs repair. There are no gutters or rain water pipes which will probably lead to dry rot, besides making the church very damp at present. In addition to proper drainage the soil should be lowered and an open paved drain formed all round the church.

Repairs, more or less, are required to the fabric, including pointing, making good to defective walls, foundations etc. I consider the cost of completing the necessary repairs not including opening out the roofs but with a new porch, and including the sums to be laid out on the chancel by the owners would amount to £700.

I am, dear Sirs,
yours truly
J. Clarke"

The church until fairly recent years was elaborately decorated for all festivals, particularly at Easter with spring flowers, and Harvest when every square inch available would be filled with fruit, flowers, hops, vegetables and greenery. Apples of every description would balance precariously on the narrow ledges round the pillars.

Rainham has never been a rich community nor has it had the benefit of local gentry, so one can imagine the impact this letter made upon the Vicar and the churchwardens. They had started work on the church in 1865 but had soon to raise money for the new school room. One realises that taxes were not so burdensome but can only admire the generosity of the people — the money was raised, not by sponsored walks or coffee mornings but by direct giving. Rainham owes a debt of gratitude to the people of the 19th century that the church was not allowed to deteriorate further.

Recently the tower has been completely overhauled and the bells made safe for future generations and in 1987 the reordering inside the church has been completed at a cost in excess of £50,000, modernising and updating the facilities to today's standards. Over the last 80 years each interior improvement has generally meant some small loss of seating so whereas in 1908 the Church recorded 800 sittings the present total is between 500 and 600. It is comforting to know that however much Rainham may change, its focal point and greatest treasure will always be its Parish Church.

THE TUFTON FAMILY

The Tufton family is first recorded as living in Sussex soon after the Norman conquest, from whence they spread into Kent and afterwards by alliances of the most honourable kind into the Northern Counties. They are supposed to have first settled in Kent in a manor called Toketon in Rainham but no trace of that name can be found here and the first real evidence is that they owned land near Sileham, Mere and Upchurch. William de Toketon was knighted by Henry III. In the reign of Elizabeth I a survey of Rainham showed 8 houses and 3 quays — one of which, called Blowers Quay, was owned by John Tufton the younger who in 1575 was Sheriff of Kent, and owner by purchase of manors all over Kent. He married Olympia Bloor and through her became possessed of Bloors Place and Sileham in Rainham. Rainham was then described as a neat and agreeable village; the high road from London to Dover running through the main street, which contained several handsome houses, and one or two good inns. To Sir John Tufton fell responsibility for the north chancel or aisle of the Parish Church of Rainham, built it is supposed by his father in law, with the vault beneath, where he lies buried. This afterwards became the sepulchre of the Tufton family.

Of the monuments in the Tufton Chapel the seated one represents George Tufton, sixth son of John the second Earl of Thanet, born 30th June 1650. There are two inscriptions, one in Latin, the other in English — this tells us that at the age of 16 he was wounded in battle in Germany on 21st October 1666. Neither in France, Germany nor England could he find any cure and he died of his wounds on December 12th 1666.

The other monument depicts Nicholas Tufton (eldest brother of George) who became third Earl of Thanet and was imprisoned in the Tower of London suspected of plotting to restore Charles II to the throne. Apart from having one tenth part of his numerous estates confiscated he seems to have suffered no injury, but after three years confinement was released and lived till 1679, when he joined George in the vault.

Rainham registers contain 3 baptisms and 32 burials of members of the Tufton family — most of which were of those who died elsewhere. The last recorded is Hon. John Tufton 1799.

Another interesting monument in the floor of the chancel is the brass of William Bloor. The inscription reads: "Under this stone is buried the body of William Flower, gentleman, who died 29th December A.D. 1529, and in the 21st year of the reign of Henry VIII by the Grace of God, King of England and France, Defender of the Faith, and Lord of Ireland, on whose soul God have mercy, Amen."

The interest to historians lies in the title 'Defender of the Faith' which Henry VIII adopted before his break with Rome. This is said to be its first appearance on any memorial in the country.

Rainham Church Choir of the 1960s. Mr Freegard, the organist, may be seen on the left.

THE CHURCH TOWER

On October 20th 1791 the tower of St Margaret's Church was greatly damaged by lightning which split it for several feet and the following day it was found that the timbers were still burning. Fortunately the fire was discovered in time and the tower was repaired, but it was more than a hundred years before a lightning conductor was fitted. History repeated itself on May 9th 1872 (Ascension Day) when a storm struck the weather vane on the tower and fired the beam to which it was fixed. The resulting fire was put out by neighbours and all was left secure by 9pm, but at a little after 5 the next morning smoke was seen by Mr G. Green issuing from the belfry. The signal post at the Railway Station had been struck during the same storm.

The history of the six oldest bells is given on page 23 of 'A Picture Book of Rainham'. Before their recasting and the installing of the two smallest bells in May 1913 the Vicar, Rev. J M. Tamplin, wrote in the magazine:

"Our bells have safely reached their destination and the work is well in hand . . . and we shall expect to have them rung again for the first time on July 20th, the commemoration of our dedication. A new floor beneath the bells will have to be provided, the masonry of the tower windows will have to be attended to and we shall take occasion to attend to the stopping of the crevices in the walls of the tower before the bells return. All this will increase the expense . . . we hope to make something by the sale of the old belfry timbers and are open to receive offers from all and sundry who would like to possess pieces of the fine old wood as mementoes. Although some of the wood is very rotten and worm eaten, yet there is plenty of very sound pieces."

While the tower records are far from complete, it is interesting to note that the inaugural meeting of the Rainham Church Bellringing Society was held in the School room on Thursday January 7th 1886 with the Vicar Rev. C. Cobb in the chair. At the next meeting a heated discussion about rules for the tower caused two members to withdraw. Only one rule was recorded, as follows: "that no beer, spirituous liquor or smoking be allowed in the Belfry or Church tower." This was afterwards crossed out and it was decided to adopt the rules of Ashford Church for the Rainham society.

A Church organ was purchased in 1866 at a cost of £158 15s 0d. The debt was still not cleared in 1874 when £8 was paid towards it.

SUNDAY SCHOOL TREATS

At the turn of the century a Sunday School treat was always held in January and the pattern never varied. Here is a typical account:

"The elder children met on Wednesday and the younger on Thursday, the number being too great to be comfortably entertained at the same time. On both evenings the same programme was gone through to the evident satisfaction of the juveniles – some of the very small people being radiant with delight. Mr Longley (Schoolmaster) exhibited the magic lantern kindly lent by Mr Walter, which never appeared to greater advantage, the views coming out distinctly and several new slides having been added. At suitable intervals an orange and a bun were handed to each child and prizes were distributed to the most regular attendants."

There must be people living in Rainham who remember Sunday School treats which followed that pattern, except perhaps for the prizes which were later distributed at the Vicarage upon production of an attendance card showing enough qualifying marks.

The Choir outing was more ambitious, they were taken by train to Whitstable. Later the Sunday School also had outings to the coast.

RAINHAM VICARS

1282	Richard of St Edmunds
1310	Richard of Marverryngs
13—	Richard de Verne
1320	William de Marinham
1323	Guido de Overe
13—	Galfridas Maleys
1378	Reginald Catigo
1380	Thomas of Gloucester
——	Nicholas Chilton
1416	William Corps
1417	Thomas Skene
1418	Richard Ffrenshe
——	William Adamson
1522	John Wright
1547	John Townsley
——	John Makelyn
1562	John Dollinshed
1571	Charles Garlick
1593	R. Joy
1609 or 1610	John Grime
1644	Griffin Spencer
1645	Thomas Bladen
1656	Thomas Lamb
1662	John Campleshon
1665	William Walter
1676	Thomas Cradock
1723	Henry Shove
1772	William Tarwell
1777	James Richards
1806	Hon. Gerald Thomas Noel
1826	John Poore
1866	Augustus John Pearman
1876	Charles Cobb
1908	John Mainwaring Tamplin
1922	William Albert Richard Ball
1929	Arthur Douglas Hodgson
1939	Edward Ernest Maples Earle
1944	Frederick William Jordan
1955	James Clifford
1967	Richard Allington Smith
1979	Michael O'Connor

This photograph was taken on St Margaret's School field on July 20th 1985 (St Margaret's Day) during a Fayre, one of the many events organised to celebrate the 650th anniversary of the rededication of the Parish Church. The past and present clergy are from left to right: Rev. John Clausen, Rev. John Rawlings, Rev. Leo Laker, Rev. Brian Pearson, Rev. Michael O'Connor, Rev. Nicholas Kerr, Rev. Richard Smith, (sitting) Rev. E.E. Maples Earle and (kneeling) Roger Martin.

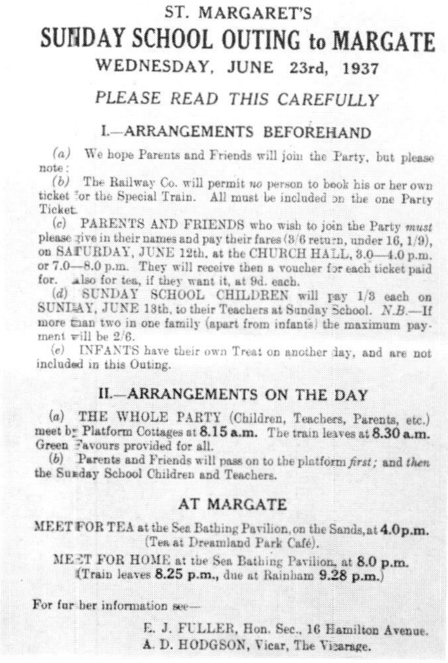

ST. MARGARET'S

SUNDAY SCHOOL OUTING to MARGATE

WEDNESDAY, JUNE 23rd, 1937

PLEASE READ THIS CAREFULLY

I.—ARRANGEMENTS BEFOREHAND

(a) We hope Parents and Friends will join the Party, but please note:

(b) The Railway Co. will permit *no* person to book his or her own ticket for the Special Train. All must be included on the one Party Ticket.

(c) PARENTS AND FRIENDS who wish to join the Party *must* please give in their names and pay their fares (3/6 return, under 16, 1/9), on SATURDAY, JUNE 12th, at the CHURCH HALL, 3.0—4.0 p.m. or 7.0—8.0 p.m. They will receive then a voucher for each ticket paid for. Also for tea, if they want it, at 9d. each.

(d) SUNDAY SCHOOL CHILDREN will pay 1/3 each on SUNDAY, JUNE 13th, to their Teachers at Sunday School. *N.B.*—If more than two in one family (apart from infants) the maximum payment will be 2/6.

(e) INFANTS have their own Treat on another day, and are not included in this Outing.

II.—ARRANGEMENTS ON THE DAY

(a) THE WHOLE PARTY (Children, Teachers, Parents, etc.) meet by Platform Cottages at **8.15 a.m.** The train leaves at **8.30 a.m.** Green Favours provided for all.

(b) Parents and Friends will pass on to the platform *first;* and *then* the Sunday School Children and Teachers.

AT MARGATE

MEET FOR TEA at the Sea Bathing Pavilion, on the Sands, at **4.0 p.m.** (Tea at Dreamland Park Café).

MEET FOR HOME at the Sea Bathing Pavilion, at **8.0 p.m.** (Train leaves **8.25 p.m.**, due at Rainham **9.28 p.m.**)

For further information see—

E. J. FULLER, Hon. Sec., 16 Hamilton Avenue.
A. D. HODGSON, Vicar, The Vicarage.

Many benefits, societies, clubs and charities are mentioned in the early records but they generally aimed at further education and the relief of the poor from harsh living standards rarely (except the Sports Clubs) purely for recreation. It was not until Scouting and Guiding led the way that many Youth groups were formed. The picture is of the Church Youth Club taken in the old Vicarage garden, apparently whilst performing a version of Robin Hood.

The Lower Rainham Road Chapel. From the 1908 directory we learn that this was a Providence United Methodist (formerly Bible Christian) Church, situated on the Lower Road at East Rainham. It was one of the oldest Nonconformist places of worship in the district, having been built in 1853. It accommodated 120 persons. Services were held at 10.45am and 6.30pm, and a Sunday School was held in connection with the Church of which Mr J. Styles was Superintendent.

Traditionally the Chapel near the bottom of Orchard Street was known as the Wakeley Chapel, having been built by a member of that family, although its correct title was The Providence Baptist Chapel. Inside may be seen a memorial with the following intriguing inscription:

"In affectionate remembrance of Thomas Stanley Wakeley, the beloved pastor of this chapel who for more than 28 years faithfully and experimentally preached to this church and congregation the glorious gospel of our Lord Jesus Christ without other reward than the blessing of God which rested on his labours. He entered into rest May 27th 1899 in his 67th year."

Apparently Mr Wakeley started his first prayer meetings in the Granary of his farm and in the Rainham Schoolroom but in 1884 built the Providence Chapel for the greater comfort of his employees, who were all expected to be regular worshippers. It is many years since religious services have been held and it is now used as a furniture store by Mr Lukehurst.

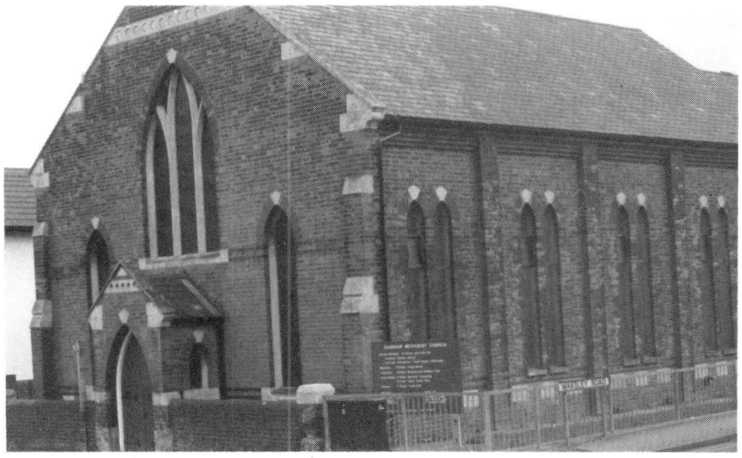

The Station Road Methodist Church was preceded by the Bible Christian Church in East Rainham. The first Minister, Rev. Fred Sparrow, moved from that church to the new one in Station Road in 1900. This is a fine building and has a very useful Sunday School hall (recently extended) at the rear. The name of Mr G.T. Mattocks will long be remembered, he served the church for 55 years as choirmaster and Sunday School Superintendent. His two sons also served the church as organist and secretary.

In 1908 there was a United Methodist Church in Ivy Street with seating accommodation for 200. A large schoolroom was to the rear. The Salvation Army also had a strong corps at Rainham, the headquarters at this time being in the Public Hall. However a piece of land had been acquired in Station Road with the idea of building a Citadel, but this could not begin until a large proportion of the cost had been collected. The Public Hall, sometimes referred to as the Institute, had been built in the middle of the 19th century just east of Orchard Street. It could comfortably accommodate 300 persons and had several ante-rooms. When the Salvation Army moved to their new Citadel in upper Station Road the hall was adapted and became the 'Cinema Royal' (more commonly known as the Bug Hutch) taking over from the original picture palace which stood on the site of the United Services Club. When the cinema closed the building became Vyes – the Kent Grocers later taken over by Liptons. It is now part of Gerald Lukehurst's furniture store and is at the moment undergoing yet more alterations to continue its chequered career. (See picture page 44.)

The United Reformed Church in Broad Walk was at the time of the 1908 directory called a Congregational Church. The directory further states that this was a modern Church containing about 300 sittings and possessing a useful pipe organ. The Congregational Sunday School was in a spacious building in Chapel Lane (now Mierscourt Road).

The final place of worship mentioned in 1908 was of the Original Peculiar People who had a meeting house in William Street.

St Matthew's Church, Wigmore – the Parish of South Gillingham.

St Augustine's Church and School, Parkwood.

Parkwood Free Church (Baptist), Parkwood Green.

Holy Trinity Church, Twydall.

St Thomas of Canterbury Roman Catholic Church, Rainham.

MODERN CHURCHES

As the population of Rainham grew with the rapid increase in house building after the Second World War new congregations developed in previously uninhabited parts of the parish. Both Twydall and Wigmore were at first satellite churches of St Margaret's but later became Parishes in their own right. Wigmore joined with Bredhurst, Parkwood and Hempstead to become the Parish of South Gillingham. Both built modern Churches after initially holding services in halls Holy Trinity at Twydall celebrates its quarter of a century this year (1987) and St Matthew's, Wigmore, was dedicated a few years later. Similarly the Roman Catholic Church, after expanding to a separate Rainham Parish in the 1950s, split again in the 1970s on completion of their new St Augustine's School and Church at Parkwood. Of the Free Churches only Station Road Methodist and the United Reformed Church at Broad Walk remain from the turn of the century, but they are joined by the Parkwood Free Church (Baptist), The Evangelical Church in Durham Road and the Rainham Evangelical Church which meets in the Community Centre at Granary Close. The Salvation Army no longer has a Corps in Rainham, the nearest being Green Street, Gillingham.

CLUBS AND SOCIETIES

The Rainham Cycling Club, according to the 1908 directory, was a large and enterprising Club with its headquarters at the Lion Hotel. The Landlord, Phil Curling, was their Treasurer and may be seen second from the right in the front row of this photograph. He was much involved in all the sporting activities that took place in Rainham. Other faces that can be identified in this 1910 picture are: Twink Barrett, Charlie Waghorn, Wally Deed, Walt Finnes, Fred Gooding, Ern Gore, Charles Moore Mark Parker, Alf Barrett, Tom Martin, Bill Lamb, Chris Horton and Jim Bing.

Most Clubs of this period seem to be dominated by the men of the village and it is not until the 1950s that we find a Ladies Darts Team from the Macklands Arms being photographed.

At this time you made your own entertainment as may be seen from the small band of assorted instruments in the photograph below.

The Rainham Bowls Club

Rabbit Shows were popular monthly events in Rainham for many years, being held in the Station Road Working Men's Club. These were partly social occasions and members used to travel long distances in order to exhibit their prize specimens at other shows.

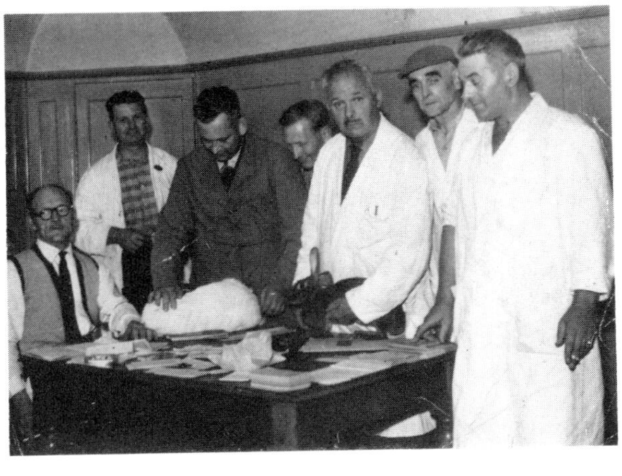

For many years Rainham had a keen following for the various Football teams, and these enjoyed a good run of success with a high degree of professionalism. Several players involved with teams in fact went on to play for league clubs. This first photograph shows an early team from the 1905/6 season with one of their trophies

Reputedly the best team Rainham ever had, this photograph shows those involved with the Rainham Football Club during the 1920s. The team used to change in the Railway Hotel and play their matches on the Recreation Ground. Large crowds were attracted to support the team and enjoy their success in various competitions. Some of the people identified in this picture are:
Back row: Gifford, Robinson, Bill Tadman, Brown, Botting.
Centre row seated: Wally Wills, Horace Moore, Bill Barrows.
Front row: 'Shrimpy' Dartnell, Bill Moore, Morgan.
The trainers were Trench Tadman and Jack Tadman.

Mr G.K. Turner (behind the boys on the right) is well remembered for his unstinting service with the children at the Church of England School. He became Headmaster after several years on the staff during which time he built up many school sports teams. These had a good deal of success in local competition. This picture shows the 1949/50 Football team outside the school building. Mr Turner was also for many years a Church warden of St Margaret's Church and also Parish Treasurer.

Maypole dancing was a traditional event at the Co-op Fete and other garden parties, but it requires much rehearsal in order to perform satisfactorily on the day. Practice sessions were sometimes held in the garden of Belmont House, opposite the Post Office, in Rainham High Street or at the Men of Kent and the actual performance was usually given on the Recreation Ground. Miss Barden is the lady in charge of this 1928 group of dancers. The festival was sometimes accompanied by a ceremony for the crowning of a May Queen.

The Berengrave Victory Fete on V.E. Day in June 1945 attracted a large crowd to watch this display by the girls of Rainham Secondary School. This formal event would today be replaced by a Majorette Marching Troupe as may be witnessed at any one of the many fetes and fairs held each year at schools and churches in Rainham. The disciplines required are basically the same and are enjoyed just as much by those participating today as they were by those who took part forty years ago.

One of the biggest boom areas in sport during the last decade has been the popularisation of mass runs. Started as serious marathon events the public at large soon appreciated the worth of this comparatively cheap but healthy way of getting into shape and jogging became an accepted fact of life. The progression to 'Fun Runs' was a natural step and these are now an established way of enjoying yourself, achieving a self-set ambition and incidentally often raising money for charity by way of sponsorship. This happy St Trinians Quintet took part in the 1986 Hempstead Valley Fun Run on May 5th (May Day Bank Holiday). They are:
Back row: Kim Thomson, Claire Pocock, Annabel Ennis.
Front row: Ashlie Murray, Nathalie Knowles.

The 1944-46 Football team from Rainham Secondary Boys School included players of remarkable calibre. During this time five boys were selected to play for the Gillingham team. One member played in the Kent Boys Football squad and one was reserve for the All England eleven. They are pictured here in the Quad at the Orchard Street School.

OUTINGS

With the advent of more reliable coaches group outings to places of interest, or sometimes just pub crawls, became popular. A selection of photographs of such outings from the many available are shown. The Mackland Arms arranged many expeditions in the 1930s when few families in Rainham owned a car.

Kemps (The Builders) works outing of the 1950s includes the following people: D. Hunt, Mr and Mrs B. Dartnell, Mr and Mrs A. Anderson, Mr Mudge, Mr and Mrs T. Crowhurst (Senior), Mr and Mrs J. Kemp, Mr and Mrs H. Samson, Mr and Mrs T. Crowhurst (Junior), Mr and Mrs A. Crowhurst and Joyce Packer.

The British Legion Outing in the late 1940s shows many local people. We have been able to identify the following: 4. Mr W. Greenstreet, 5. Des Norris, 7. Mr Harris (from Hartlip), 9. Mrs Harris (from Hartlip), 10. Rose Gransden, 11. Miss Temple, 12. Westo Gransden, 14. Mr Gransden, 16. Mrs Mortimar, 17. Jessie Mortimar (daughter of No.16), 18. Jacky Moore, 19. Mr Jones, 20. Mrs W. Greenstreet, 22. Mrs Brunger, 23. George Henthorn, 24. Mr Nicholls, 25. Mr Henthorn (Senior), 26. Les Bryant, 29. Mrs Clark (from Newington), 30. Leon Jones, 33. Mr Morgan, 34. Clara Allan, 35. Bert Allan, 36. Albert Moore, 37. Mrs Ellen Gransden, 38. Mrs Bernard Knight, 39. Dolly Morgan, 40. Mrs Nicholls, 41. Mrs Cecilia Henthorn, 42. Mrs Henthorn (Senior), 44. Margaret Jones, 45. Mr Wills, 47. Peggy Temple, 48. Gillian Gransden, 49. ? Moore, 50. Ron Cook, 51. 'Granny' Moore, 52. Fred Webb, 53. Joan Webb, 54. Georgie Bates, 55. Dicky Bates, 56. Mrs Beams, 57. Bernard Knight, 58. Mr Beams, 59. Alice Bates, 61. Ivy Harris, 64. Phil Ponds, 65. Mr Clark.

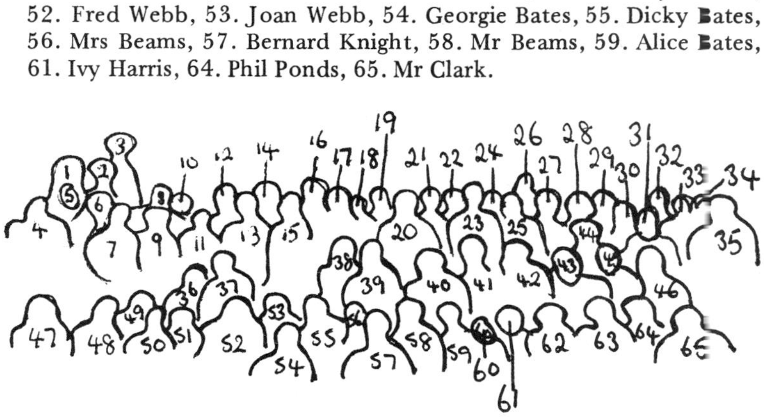

The Mackland Arms Outing 1935.
In coach: Moore, Morgan, Foster, Willis, Murton, Smith, O'Brien, Blundy, Nutting, Smith, Blackman.
Centre: Evans, Smith, Smith, Hughes, Ashdown, Ringham, Gillman, Barker, Dalby, Dalby, Gillman.
Still, Chapman, Blundy, Sutton, Pointer, Pointer, Keutinus, Blundy, Blundy, Gowers, Skinner.
Front: Still, Skinner, Tadman, Still, Still, Platt, Platt, Blackman, Ashby, Ringham.

PLAYS AND PRODUCTIONS

This photograph is of the Crowning Ceremony of Rainham's Darby and Joan Christmas Queen in December 1952. The Ceremony took place on the back of a lorry supplied by Mr E.H. Nicholls in the forecourt of the Cricketers public house.

From left to right: Mrs Grace Norris attending the Queen, eighty-seven-year-old Queen Mrs Clara (Betty) Stockbridge, Mrs G.M. Pinfold performing the crowning, Mrs Ada Philpott another attendant, George Mattocks, the Rev. F.W. Jordan, Mrs Choules, Pastor F.G. Crane, Mrs Hopkins.

Also Christmas 1952, this photograph is of the Camp School pantomime, Aladdin, performed in the School hall. The Camp School was a temporary post war emergency measure to cope with the 'bulge years' of birth rate (1945 onwards) caused by the demobilisation of the forces who immediately returned home to their wives or married their sweethearts! The Camp was so called because it occupied an old wartime Army Camp site (now Bettescombe Road). The Army huts and buildings were transformed into classrooms and a huge hangar type hall and canteen (at least they seemed huge to this five year old who attended the school as an infant). The School continued in an ever more dilapidated state until the end of the 1950s when the Fairview Schools were built and all the children and staff transferred to a new purpose-built complex. Not all were pleased however as this was a long walk for the Arthur Road area children who had been used to a school on their doorstep.

A Nativity play presented by the Women's Fellowship in (about) 1947. The play was produced by Mrs Rayner and Miss Cox. Those participating were as follows:
Shepherds: Mrs Fairey, Mrs Lazenby, Mrs Hollingsworth and Mrs Nicholls. The boy shepherds were the Rev. Mitchell's two sons. Joseph was Mrs I. Wall. The kings: Mrs Choules, Mrs Hopkins and the page was Mrs Hollingsworth's adopted son. The angels included Mrs Choules daughter, ? Garlinge, ? Smith, Pat and Elizabeth Barrow and Janice Hawkins. The grandmother was Miss Norwood.

1985 PAGEANT

In 1985 as part of the 650th anniversary of the rededication of St Margaret's Church, an elaborate pageant was written by Miss Audrey Perkyns and produced by Miss Irene Cox. The pageant, which took many months of preparation, was mimed to pre-recorded tapes and performed on July 15th at 8.00pm in the church. Six scenes from the history of Rainham are reproduced as a flavour of this mammoth undertaking.

The Romans: Centurion: Brian Salter, Tribune: Terry Clare, Soldiers: Nigel Byott, Phil Smith, Richard Davies and Jonathan Noakes.

Mediaeval Times 1474: Sir Thomas Leger: Brian Bailey, Page: Fiona Pierce, Lady Ann: Pam Bailey, Maids: Sharon Davies and Charlotte Anthony, Vicar: Terry Clare, Churchwardens: Dennis Connor and Ron Baker, Villagers: Rachel Meinertzhagen, Mary Ann Garner and Marion Byott, John: Mary Trice, Mason: Peter Gray, Children: Jenny and Emma Gray.

Unveiling the Tufton Statue 1671: Nicholas, Earl of Thanet: Ken Smith, Lady Margaret: Ellen Stringer, Maid: Sally Muggeridge, Vicar: Morton Jarvis. (For a short history of the Tufton family see page 16.)

Meeting of the Church Council 1766: Vicar: Ron Jennings, John Wakeley: David Noakes, John Fryer: Peter Gray, William Hayles: John Anthony, William Hatch: Bob Douglas, Isaac Wildish: Graham Starkey, Bob Turner: Margaret Buss, Dame Brown: Hilary Noakes.

The Brickies late 19th century: The cast for the Brickies scene included the following people: Matthew Still, Christopher Still, Tracy Hobson, Jonathan Noakes, David Wickenden, Chris Divers, Alan Wildridge, Dannan Whyte, Simon Halstead and Simon O'Connor.

The Final Scene — Looking to the Future: Authority — Mayor: Stella Bostock, Councillors: Jo Myers, Ethel Blake, Marian Cornish and Rosemary Herrod. Newcomers: Jim Bellars, Petula Tombs Conservationists: Audrey Hunt, Wanda Jay.

VISITORS TO RAINHAM

The field behind the High Street shops from the old School playground to Holding Street was often loaned by its owner for various functions. On this occasion it was host to a travelling evangelist who lived in his caravan and held meetings in the nearby marquee. The van was liberally inscribed with religious slogans. 'We Preach Christ Crucified', 'The Wages of Sin is Death', 'Salvation is the Lord' and 'The Blood of Jesus Christ God's Son Cleanseth us from all Sin' are those which may be seen.

The opening ceremony on the first day of the Gillingham Park Fete, which was held on Wednesday and Thursday July 8th and 9th in 1936, was performed by Jim and Amy Mollison, the world famous aviators (better known perhaps as Amy Johnson and her husband). In these days the schools had a holiday for fruit picking in July, hence a midweek fete, returned to lessons in August but had a further holiday in September for hop picking. On Thursday the fete was opened by the famous film star Mr Leslie Fuller. The price of admission to the park for this grand event was Adults: 3d, Children: 1d. The picture shows Amy Johnson with Councillor Tye, who was Mayor of Gillingham at the time. The Mayoress presented Amy with a silver salver as a memento of her visit to Gillingham, which may now be seen at the Amy Johnson Museum, Sewerby Hall, Bridlington, Yorkshire. The honoured guests were entertained to luncheon at the Central Hotel, Rainham Road and just prior to this the procession toured Rainham.

United Kingdom Band of Hope Union.

PATRON:
HIS MAJESTY THE KING.

Certificate of Merit
awarded to
Leslie Eccles
for Excellence in Reporting a Lecture
on the
Hygiene of Food & Drink.

U·K·B·OF·H·U· FIRST YEAR

OFFICES OF THE UNION,- 59 & 60, OLD BAILEY, E.C.4

PRESIDENT

DATE 30 MAR 1936 Charles Harvey
LECTURER

A regular visitor to schools in the area was Mr Charles Harvey who was permitted to lecture the children on the dangers of the misuse of alcohol. By 1935 he must have been a very old man for he seemed old to his prewar audiences, also the title of his lecture must have broadened if it was really on the hygiene of food and drink. Perhaps by then he had stopped illustrating his lecture by dropping a worm into a glass of alcohol to show the dire results of strong drink, however the certificate of merit was still awarded to those who achieved excellence in reporting his lecture. Perhaps they all did.

In July 1921 the Duke of York was scheduled to drive through Rainham on his way to an engagement in Dover. Unfortunately the entourage took the wrong route from London driving through Maidstone instead and missing the excited schoolchildren all waiting to cheer him along Rainham High Street. Hurried re-arrangements were made however and he did eventually return along the planned route. How long the children waited in the morning is not remembered.

GARDEN PARTIES AND FETES

Garden parties and fetes have long been a feature of life in Rainham. These were as much social occasions for entertainment and enjoyment as for fund raising. Events changed little from year to year and everyone knew just what to expect.

The Co-op Fete was preceded by a carnival procession with many floats suitably decorated and the accompanying persons in fancy dress. These three photographs show some of the entries in the 1920s

A horse drawn cart on its way to the Recreation Ground outside the White Horse at the top of Station Road.

The 'woman' on the left in the photograph above is in fact Mr Samson, who was manager of the Rainham Co-op High Street branch for many years.

Mr Samson in this picture is dressed as a policeman in a borrowed uniform. Great fun was had by all and everyone young and old joined in the annual event.

Until the introduction of Earl Haig's 'Poppy Day' Rainham's street collection was confined to the weekly Salvation Army services and the annual Alexandra Rose Day collection. This was a very well organised affair, seen here in preparation, run by the ladies of the village and their children. The Misses Quinnel were largely responsible for the sale which raised money for the Queen Alexandra Nursing Association.

EIIR
Coronation
1953

OFFICIAL PROGRAMME
of
RAINHAM
CORONATION
CELEBRATIONS

★

Coronation Celebrations Committee

Chairman—Councillor P. F. Cooper Vice-Chairman—R. Lucas, Esq.
Secretary—H. C. Bassadona, Esq. Hon. Treasurer—J. E. Lewis, Esq.

Organising Sub-Committees

Coronation Day Committee—R. Lucas, Esq., Chairman
Carnival Committee—G. House, Esq., Chairman
Decoration Committee—Dr. G. O. S. Reid, Chairman
Dance and Entertainment Committee—A. H. Stapley, Esq., Chairman

Panda Press, Rainham

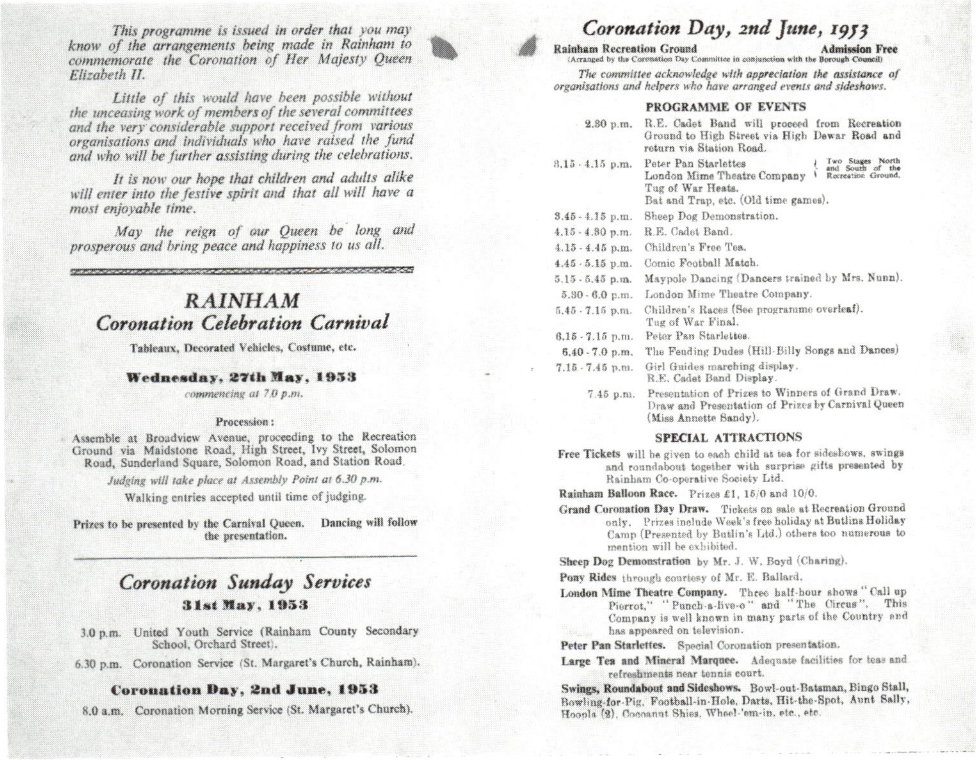

This programme is issued in order that you may know of the arrangements being made in Rainham to commemorate the Coronation of Her Majesty Queen Elizabeth II.

Little of this would have been possible without the unceasing work of members of the several committees and the very considerable support received from various organisations and individuals who have raised the fund and who will be further assisting during the celebrations.

It is now our hope that children and adults alike will enter into the festive spirit and that all will have a most enjoyable time.

May the reign of our Queen be long and prosperous and bring peace and happiness to us all.

RAINHAM
Coronation Celebration Carnival

Tableaux, Decorated Vehicles, Costume, etc.

Wednesday, 27th May, 1953
commencing at 7.0 p.m.

Procession:
Assemble at Broadview Avenue, proceeding to the Recreation Ground via Maidstone Road, High Street, Ivy Street, Solomon Road, Sunderland Square, Solomon Road, and Station Road.

Judging will take place at Assembly Point at 6.30 p.m.

Walking entries accepted until time of judging.

Prizes to be presented by the Carnival Queen. Dancing will follow the presentation.

Coronation Sunday Services
31st May, 1953

3.0 p.m. United Youth Service (Rainham County Secondary School, Orchard Street).
6.30 p.m. Coronation Service (St. Margaret's Church, Rainham).

Coronation Day, 2nd June, 1953

8.0 a.m. Coronation Morning Service (St. Margaret's Church).

Coronation Day, 2nd June, 1953

Rainham Recreation Ground **Admission Free**
(Arranged by the Coronation Day Committee in conjunction with the Borough Council)

The committee acknowledge with appreciation the assistance of organisations and helpers who have arranged events and sideshows.

PROGRAMME OF EVENTS

2.30 p.m.	R.E. Cadet Band will proceed from Recreation Ground to High Street via High Dewar Road and return via Station Road.
3.15 - 4.15 p.m.	Peter Pan Starlettes / London Mime Theatre Company (Two Stages North and South of the Recreation Ground.) Tug of War Heats. Bat and Trap, etc. (Old time games).
3.45 - 4.15 p.m.	Sheep Dog Demonstration.
4.15 - 4.30 p.m.	R.E. Cadet Band.
4.15 - 4.45 p.m.	Children's Free Tea.
4.45 - 5.15 p.m.	Comic Football Match.
5.15 - 5.45 p.m.	Maypole Dancing (Dancers trained by Mrs. Nunn).
5.30 - 6.0 p.m.	London Mime Theatre Company.
5.45 - 7.15 p.m.	Children's Races (See programme overleaf). Tug of War Final.
6.15 - 7.15 p.m.	Peter Pan Starlettes.
6.40 - 7.0 p.m.	The Feuding Dudes (Hill-Billy Songs and Dances)
7.15 - 7.45 p.m.	Girl Guides marching display. R.E. Cadet Band Display.
7.45 p.m.	Presentation of Prizes to Winners of Grand Draw. Draw and Presentation of Prizes by Carnival Queen (Miss Annette Sandy).

SPECIAL ATTRACTIONS

Free Tickets will be given to each child at tea for sideshows, swings and roundabout together with surprise gifts presented by Rainham Co-operative Society Ltd.

Rainham Balloon Race. Prizes £1, 15/0 and 10/0.

Grand Coronation Day Draw. Tickets on sale at Recreation Ground only. Prizes include Week's free holiday at Butlins Holiday Camp (Presented by Butlin's Ltd.) others too numerous to mention will be exhibited.

Sheep Dog Demonstration by Mr. J. W. Boyd (Charing).

Pony Rides through courtesy of Mr. E. Ballard.

London Mime Theatre Company. Three half-hour shows "Call up Pierrot," "Punch-a-live-o" and "The Circus". This Company is well known in many parts of the Country and has appeared on television.

Peter Pan Starlettes. Special Coronation presentation.

Large Tea and Mineral Marquee. Adequate facilities for teas and refreshments near tennis court.

Swings, Roundabout and Sideshows. Bowl-out-Batsman, Bingo Stall, Bowling-for-Pig, Football-in-Hole, Darts, Hit-the-Spot, Aunt Sally, Hoopla (2), Coconut Shies, Wheel-'em-in, etc., etc.

In common with most of the British Isles and Commonwealth, Rainham had grand plans for celebrating the Coronation of Queen Elizabeth II on Tuesday 2nd June 1953. Fortunately these began well before the actual day as that dawned wet and cold, enough to dampen anyone's festive spirit. Most of the population were gathered in the homes of those who possessed televisions for the morning's live coverage of this momentous event. I must confess that I remember little of the historic occasion except frequent visits to the window to see if it had stopped raining and being noisily 'shushed' every time I opened my mouth. Eventually the broadcast finished and the rain more or less ceased and Rainham spent the remainder of the day celebrating on the Rec.

A fancy dress parade during a fete on the Recreation Ground. Behind the contestants in this photograph you can see the 'prefabs' of Wakeley Road. These were prefabricated houses which were built very quickly after the war to house the homecoming forces and their families. A great deal of housing was needed quickly to replace all the bombed out areas in the cities. Rainham had several estates of the prefabs which were built with the idea of lasting ten years during which time it was imagined sufficient permanent housing would be built. Thirty years on and some of the prefabs were still in use, but I think all have now gone.

All the schools in the area now hold their own Summer Fete, usually organised by the Parent Teachers Association. These are very successful social occasions and provide welcome boosts to the school fund. Often the money raised is used for optional extras the school would not otherwise be able to afford, such as learner swimming pools and computers. St George can be seen confronting the dragon at this, St Margaret's School, Fete held in July 1981.

RAINHAM AND DISTRICT CO-OPERATIVE SOCIETY

One of the earliest photographs of the Co-op is this of 1911 taken of the Station Road shop to show the Christmas display. The business had actually started on the other side of Station Road and moved across on completion of this building, constructed for the Co-operative Society by Kemp Brothers (Builders). Mr Barden, a local man, was voted by the shareholders to be the first President of the society. In this photograph may be seen (from left to right) Hodge, Bert Col, the people either side of the Managing Secretary, A.W. Barnes who is wearing a dark suit, are unnamed, then Mr G. Coltrup, Freddy Ockwell (in the centre), Mr Trafford Tom Mattocks, N. Black and H. Samson.

By 1924 the date of this next photograph the Co-op had undergone a facelift. A glass canopy had been constructed along the length of the shop front covering the pavement. This enabled elaborate displays to be staged outside the shop, such as this one for Libbys tinned goods. Mr Samson, at that time Manager of the Household Department, had lent the props for the display and was invited to pose in the picture. Miss Violet Manser (later Mrs Kitchenham) with a borrowed child completed the scene. The school across the road can be seen reflected in the window.

(Below left)
Rainham and District Co-operative Society Grocery Department staff in front of their Christmas display December 1933. They are from left to right: Alf Champion, Ben Rodwell, Percy Major, Reg Lucas, Joe Cox, Foulsher, Mugouton, Doug Evers, and Norrington. The shop front had been altered again in 1932 and the canopy removed.
(Below right)
The Station Road Co-op as it appeared from 1932 until it was converted to a supermarket in the 1960s. The building has now been sold and subdivided into three smaller shop units.

The High Street branch of the Co-op was built by Kemps in 1928. It has a large hall upstairs reached either from the small door which may be seen in the picture of the 1935 addition or from a flight of stone stairs around the back to the right hand side of the building. The hall was much used for all kinds of local events until it was declared unsafe in the late 1950s. Part has now been incorporated into the shop by the addition of an inside staircase. (The hall may be seen more clearly in a picture on page 39.) This picture, taken soon after the opening in 1928, shows a competition window display on the right designed by Fred Mattocks. From left to right in the picture are: W. Samson, C. Gooding, H. Budds, A. Mattocks and W. Costin.

In 1935 land next door to the Co-op building in the High Street was purchased from Wakeleys and an extension to the shop was built. This remains very similar in appearance today. Church House, which can just be glimpsed, has long since been demolished leaving an ugly gap which has still to be filled.

RAINHAM LIBRARY

Until the 20th century people knew their station in life and for the most part stayed in it and felt no shame in singing about the rich man in his castle with the poor man at his gate. When Mrs Pearman, the Vicar's wife, started the lending library in 1869 Rule 1 decreed that subscribers belonging to the working class should pay 1d per month or one shilling a year while tradesmen and others should pay 2s 6d per year, to be entitled to borrow one volume weekly. This library was contained in the Infants School room and consisted largely of books donated by the Society for Promoting Christian Knowledge. From a list of 221 books I have quoted every 10th book to give an idea of what was on offer.

1. Travels in Denmark etc	121. Mirage of Life
11. Motherless Lads	131. Conversion of St Paul
21. Travels in Asia	141. Characters of the Reformation
31. Peoples Magazine	151. Outlines of English History
41. Life of James David	161. Christian Missions
51. Substances used as Food	171. Life of God in the Soul
61. Pennywise and Pound Foolish	181. Old Humphries Country Pictures
71. Book of Houses	191. Britons and Saxons
81. Field and Garden	201. History of the Reformation
91. Happy Land	211. Pilgrim Street
101. Summers Lectures Vol.3	221. White Moss Rose
111. Anxious Enquirer	

Later on as more books were added a few more novels appear in the list such as 'Swiss Family Robinson' and 'The Lamplighter' but only those of a very educational and improving sort.

By the early part of the 20th century the library had moved from the schoolroom to the ground floor of the Temperance Hotel in Station Road. It was still only open on Monday afternoons until 9pm, the other room being the reading room where newspapers and chairs were provided for the studious. The library under the parish council stayed here until Gillingham took over Rainham and moved the books to an empty shop (now Kent Reliance) in the High Street. By that time there was a very good selection of books and no fees. The children's section was very firmly controlled by the librarian, Miss Cremer. In 1961 the excellent modern library was built in Birling Avenue and is now administered by Kent County Council.

1st Rainham Brownies originally met on Saturday mornings in the old School Hall at the top of Station Road. Here they may be seen in 1924 with their Brown Owl, Miss Elsie Johnson, at the back and her two assistants Lena Goodger (left) and Flossie Buck (right). The Brownies were:

Back row: S. Trice, C. Warren, R. Elvy, I. Hughes, L.L. Barrett, K. Boon, M. Dye, N. Lee.

Centre row: S. Lee, M. Hedges, E. Taylor, M. Moore, M. Hyland, D. Day, D. Dye, S. Brockman.

Front row: I. Green, Q. Brown, F. Cramp, ?, D. Howland, S. Blueit, ?, S. Todd, M Chapman, K. Holdstock.

YOUTH GROUPS

After the first world war Youth Groups and other clubs and societies began to flourish in Rainham. A small selection of some of the activities on offer are shown on this page.

Here the 1st Rainham Rangers of the early 1930s enjoy a tea party with their Captain Mrs Rayner probably in her garden in Longley Road.

Also from the thirties this group of lads from the St Margaret's Youth Club with the Vicar, Rev. A.D. Hodgson (playing darts). The club met in the hall of the old school at the top of Station Road.

This photograph shows a unit of the Girls Brigade from the 1950s who used to meet in the Methodist Sunday School Room in Station Road.

Old Time dancing in the Co-op hall.

WELFARE IN THE 19TH CENTURY

Traditionally the Church was responsible for the care of the poor of its parish and it is from Church records that we learn how much was done by voluntary subscription before the state took on the responsibility.

In 1870 the Nourishment Club raised £8 10s 0d and spent it on food for 28 mothers. The rules were as follows:

1. An annual subscription of 5s entitles the subscriber to one recommendation.
2. Annual subscriptions of 10s and £1 entitle the subscriber to one or two and 3 or 4, according to the state of the funds of the society.
3. Any woman residing in Rainham is eligible for the tickets providing she can produce a recommendation from a subscriber.
4. The tickets are not given for the first child after marriage.
5. Three sets of tickets are given to each woman, each set being equal to 1lb of mutton, 2 quarts of beer, and 6d worth of oatmeal, sugar and spice, with the last set given in money.
6. The sum given to each woman being 6s 6d: the 1s 6d over the amount of the subscription is paid by the subscriptions of those who do not care for recommendations.
7. Recommendations not given away in the first year can be given in the 2nd, 3rd or 4th years etc.
8. An additional recommendation can be had at any time on payment of 5s.

Rainham Blanket Society

This was run on similar lines to the Nourishment Club except that the recipients of the blankets had to have paid 1s for an entitlement. In 1869 subscriptions were £12 12s 0d, members paid £1 19s 0d and the number of blankets distributed was 39. The blankets were only distributed on one day a year, St Thomas's Day (December 21st) at 8.00 am at Bloors Place.

Rainham Clothing and Coal Club

Again we have a list of subscribers, usually the same names, who gave a total of £15 in 1869. In this club members paid a weekly sum amounting to £51 14s 9d in 1869 for clothing and £14 5s 7d for coal. Sunday School children were allowed to hold clothing cards and accounted for £9 6s 7d. A bonus of 2d for adults and 3d for children was added to each shilling on the cards. No money was accepted from children who had not attended Sunday School for the previous week. The suppliers of clothing and coal had to be subscribers.

During 1870 and 1871 there was a great deal of poverty among the people of Rainham and a long list of subscribers gave sums of £1 to 2s 6d to a Soup Kitchen fund. In 1871 £15 2s 6d was raised in this way to which was added the proceeds of the penny readings £1 12s 6d.

Penny Readings

The penny readings were quite an institution in the parish, and probably started up very simply. By 1872 however they were held monthly during the winter and were well supported both by the working class who paid their penny and the better educated who took part in the entertainment – a varied programme being enjoyed by all.

Rainham TOC H in the 1930s
Back row: W.A. Cook, S. Costen, T. Dennis, A.J. Ramsdale.
Centre: ?, W. Russell, Rev. A.D. Hodgson, E. Sargent, W.A. Dennis, P. Riley, A.E. Gleadle.
Front: W. Edwards, Col. H.E. Day, E.J. Ready, W.J. Smith, W.G. Thomas, A.R. Thompson, Comdr H.J. Harvey, G.H. Cumberworth, K. Oldland.

A parade of Special Constables after attending the Congregational Church 8th June 1942/3? led by Schoolmaster Mr W.J. Smith.

The party held at St Margaret's Hall in 1945 to welcome home Rainham's ex-European Prisoners of War which was arranged by the local Red Cross. At the time others were still held by the Japanese.

TRANSPORT

These pictures provide an insight into the choice of transport available at the turn of the century. Walking was of course the most common, also the cheapest but slowest way to get about, but increasingly bicycles became a familiar sight. For longer adventures there were the trams and trains but these journeys often involved long walks at each end of the expedition. Horse drawn transport was still the most common way to carry most goods and people. If it were not for the Lion with its notice 'You may telephone from here' a newcomer would not recognise this as Rainham. The vicarage on the left, Quinnells Grocers shop, Belmont House and the next three shops on the right are all gone. Dr Webster owned the first car in Rainham and the little black cab looks very like the fever cart that conveyed diphtheria and scarlet fever patients to Keycol Hill Isolation Hospital.

The building opposite the Lion with the oriel window was the vicarage. It is unusual for a village to have a parsonage and a vicarage but such is the case in Rainham. The original parsonage was built by the Abbot of Leeds for the parson of the newly dedicated Church in the 14th century. Henry VIII appropriated all properties belonging to Leeds Abbey and so the parsonage and 18 acres of land became the property of the King. Queen Elizabeth I let it for £16 a year to the Moyle family who eventually bought it with its remaining tythes. Without a home for their Vicar the parishioners built a vicarage next door to the parsonage. This state of affairs continued until about 30 years ago when a new vicarage was built next to church path in Broadview Avenue and the old one was sold to the Post Office, who demolished the old building and built a sorting office in the grounds. The parsonage which dates from the time of Queen Anne remains. (See page 10 of 'Picture Book of Old Rainham'.)

Mr Lockyer of Meres Court (spelling from the cart) was the local milkman. Here are two views of his cart after it had been in for repair at Kemsley's forge.

This photograph shows the first tram to run into Rainham in 1906. Apart from the historic interest there are two points worth noting. Before the war there was always a policeman standing at the junction of Station Road and the High Street. This was not only to control traffic but to give a point of contact for the public so that crime could be nipped in the bud by an early warning to the offender or a word in the ear of a parent who would then keep the youngster on the straight and narrow. The 'long arm of the law' could see all from this vantage point! The other interest in the picture is in the three sailors — both soldiers and sailors were a common sight in Rainham when Chatham was a Garrison town.

Sadly the age of the tram ended and these photographs show all the rolling stock lined up on the tracks opposite the Star Hotel, Watling Street, ready for sale at I believe £5 each to anyone who wanted one. What you did with a redundant tram or how you even took it away remains a mystery, but one possible suggestion is that they were converted and used as holiday homes at local seaside resorts such as Allhallows or as a temporary residence on one of the wooded country plots at that time being sold in Wigmore and the surrounding area. The advertisement on the side of each tram in the lower picture is the same. It reads "Wallace Hewett Tailoring 1,3,5,7 Rock Avenue, Gillingham." The Dockyard trams have more variety in their advertisements. Some of these read: "Oxford and Cambridge Cream for Shoes", "OK Sauce" and "Millennium Flour and Wrapped Bread". This photograph is dated 30th September 1930.

An excellent close up view of the Rainham—Town Hall (Chatham) tram at the terminus in Rainham High Street. Trams had no need to turn round, the driver simply moved to the other end for the return journey while the conductor turned the overhead arm to the power supply the other way. Stopping in the centre of the road in this manner soon caused traffic congestion — not to mention a certain amount of danger to passengers — and the track was therefore subsequently continued around the corner into Station Road.

ACCIDENTS

Life expectancy was short in the 19th century as may be seen from the lists of burials recorded in the Church registers. In 1868 of thirty two burials 16 were children under four years of age and 6 of people over 60. Many fatal and serious accidents are described. Some are as follows:

April 11th 1867 — George Richardson fell from a barge in Rainham Quay and was drowned.

April 15th 1867 — Burial of Annie Goodwin age 2½ years. Killed by being knocked down by a horse and cart in Station Road.

Friday evening August 9th 1867 — A man named Curtis, native of Sittingbourne, was killed when unloading empty casks opposite Mr Moss's shop. A cask rolled over and frightened the horse which bolted and threw Mr Curtis out of the van. On the advice of Mr Everest he was conveyed the same evening to St Bartholomew's Hospital where he died the following morning.

April 29th 1868 — Alfred Rayfield aged 9 years was run over at the corner of the lane leading from the turnpike road to Lower Rainham. He died in St Bartholomew's Hospital on May 4th. It is remarkable that seeing his danger he had the presence of mind to throw the baby he was carrying from his arms and thus saved its life.

The next day on April 30th there was a serious fire in the afternoon on the premises attached to the White Horse Inn. "All classes readily joined in hearty efforts to check the progress of what might have been a dreadful calamity, and there being a good supply of water at hand the flames were quickly subdued before the arrival of the engine from Chatham, which was speedily on the road, but not before part of the outbuildings belonging to the inn and Dr Knights stables had been consumed. The property was fortunately insured."

T. Standen & Sons of Sittingbourne began this service bus between Sittingbourne and Rainham late in 1913. This photograph was taken in Newington.

An early Maidstone & District open top coach used for an outing to Brighton from Rainham in 1919. The party was organised by Mr Holding of the Rainham Brotherhood. The hood of the coach, which may be seen neatly furled at the back, could be used if necessary but had a rather claustrophobic effect on the passengers. One wonders how comfortable a ride it was on the solid tyres.

Rather larger organised parties set off from Rainham in later years as may be seen from this line of six Maidstone & District coaches ready for departure in the High Street.

ACCIDENTS cont

January 26th 1873 – James Mark aged 17 years, a quiet civil lad, drowned when a barge in which he served as mate was run down at Tilbury.
1873 was a sad year for the Castle family of the Lion public house. On August 9th the awfully sudden death of Mr F. Castle aged 27 years of the Lion was announced leaving a widow and young children and in October it was learned that Edwin Castle aged 21 had been washed overboard from the SS Bundaleer at Lat 40S Long 84E.

In October 1875 a young man named George Gooding aged 25 years lost his life in Mr Watson's Oasthouse.
Drownings from barges are frequently mentioned and these continued up to about 1930 when Mr Mark Ransley lost his life when his barge foundered. Run away horses accounted for the majority of road accidents, but apparently only one fatality is remembered in what one would consider the more dangerous motor age. Frank Wade aged 6 years was knocked down and killed in London Road in March 1916.

Horse drawn vehicles gave way to motorised transport and lorries, such as these in A.V. Stinton's yard at the end of Longley Road, became a common sight. The building was destroyed by fire in September 1924.

A steam lorry belonging to the British Standard Cement Company loading from the barges at Motney. In the picture may be seen from left to right: W.H. Reynolds, Horace Moore (Mate), W. Frid and W. Buley (Driver). In order to replace worn solid tyres the lorry had to be driven to London and the whole operation took four days. It was on the back of this lorry that the War Memorial was transported to its present site in 1920 after it arrived by train at Rainham Station.

The London to Dover rail line through Rainham was electrified in 1959 and since then we have not seen this sight of a steam train thundering through Rainham Station. The large Oast House and store were purchased from Wakeleys by the Rainham and Wigmore Community Association in 1971 and have since been converted into a Community Centre. The old cottages were subsequently demolished and replaced by the new houses of Granary Close.

HOT SUMMERS

In the 1860s and 70s there seem to have been a series of very hot summers which were inevitably accompanied by much illness particularly among the very young. In August 1869 the annual breaking up treat at the school was cancelled owing to sickness and in that month the burial register read as follows:

August	1	Charles Hopper	aged 10 months
	2	Lavinia Smith	3 months
	9	Ann Tree	69 years
	13	Ann Janet Macbride	14 months
	13	John Edward Reader	1½ years
	14	Thomas Edward Everden	2 months
	15	Rachel Sage	9 months
	27	Stephen Elvy	3 years

At that time the total population of Rainham was less than 2,000.

FROM THE TOP OF THE CHURCH TOWER

A series of pictures of Rainham from the top of the Church Tower. The early ones were taken by Mr Samson in May 1930 and the later ones are about forty years after.

This is the group who were on the tower with Mr Samson.

From left to right: H. Ransley. W. Costen, A. Coppin, C. Gooding, S. Reeves, S. Mattocks and C. Belsey — the Captain of the Bell Ringers, who opened up the tower and accompanied the party of workers from Rainham Co-op.

Looking West. The large building on the left is the Public Hall, at this time converted to a cinema (see pages 19 and 44). Holding Street has been newly constructed beyond the field on the right but open space still remains to the south of the A2, shortly to become Thames Avenue.

Looking North-East. In the foreground the Co-op clock (which was removed in the 60s) may be seen and then the old parsonage and the vicarage (see page 34) with their large gardens. All the open space has now disappeared under housing.

Looking East. This view towards Moor Street shows the orchards and fields which still surround Rainham on its eastern border, but all the nearest areas to the centre have now been developed.

POPULATION OF RAINHAM

In 1821 the population of Rainham was 1,031 living in 164 dwellings. This crept up slowly for the next 50 years reaching 1,500 by 1871, but then the rapid rises began, reaching 3,800 people by 1901 and at the time of these 1930 photographs the population of Rainham stood at 5,900. Tremendous leaps were now made to reach a total of around 30,000 people in 1971 at the time of these later views and today (1987) Rainham has a population of over 40,000 (including Parkwood, Hempstead and Wigmore).

The 1930 view of the churchyard. Much of this orchard has just recently, within the last year, been developed with housing although the land adjacent to the churchyard and has been given to the church. The by-pass has been proposed for at least the last 40 years and there is still no immediate danger of its being built!

The High Street showing the Co-op Hall above the shop.

Town houses in Church Mews.

Broad Walk

AGRICULTURE

The 1907 Boxing Day shoot for rabbits at Matts Hill, Rainham. The men were from left to right: Mr Rayner, Mr Clarke (Grigsby Lodge), B. Clarke, Jim Clarke (seated), Mr Dobson (who it may just be seen had a hook instead of one hand), H.G. Samson (seated, father to the Mr Samson who now lives in Broadview Avenue), and H.G. Samson, his grandfather.

Hops have all but disappeared from Rainham in the last few years, but before this mechanical picking had replaced the old hand picking methods in the 1950s and 60s. The use of stilts, however, for stringing the hops in spring continued. This photograph of the man on stilts was taken in April 1976 in Meresborough Road. Nowadays you probably need to visit the Beltring Hop Museum at Paddock Wood in order to experience the old time flavour of the Kentish Hop Gardens.

Mr Kemsley (blacksmith) of the Orchard Street Forge is standing proudly by what he thought, at the time the photograph was taken, was the last old Kent plough he would repair. However as this was 1939 and war was declared soon afterwards he actually repaired many more for the local farmers, when modern machinery became very difficult to obtain.

Harvesting has undergone equally rapid development from the highly labour intensive hand cutting by scythe, through this early tractor driven cutter to the early combine harvester (illustrated) and finally the modern giants of machinery we see in the fields today.

One of the few things that as yet cannot be mechanised is cherry picking. Trees cannot be satisfactorily dwarfed as have pears and apples to enable much easier picking from the ground or low ladders, and the cherry harvest has therefore to be gathered in just the same way as it always has been from the great long ladders that stretch right up into the enormous trees. It is the cherry orchards that still provide the most spectacular sight in blossom time each spring and fortunately, despite all the problems they bring for the farmer, we still have several orchards around Rainham. This earliest photograph of cherry pickers (about 1900) includes Bill Hales, Eliza Davidson, Mrs Andrews and her daughter, Mr Miles and C. Davison.

Cherry pickers in the 1940s in Scotts orchard. Mrs Moore (standing beneath the ladder) who worked for Scotts for 50 years is with Mrs Ward who is picking from the ground.

Soft fruit also defies the machine but farmers are increasingly overcoming this problem by opening their fields to the public as 'Pick Your Own' Centres. However some gangs of women are still employed to pick the cream of the crop to be sold at market. Here is a gang of gooseberry pickers on Wakeleys farm in the 1930s.

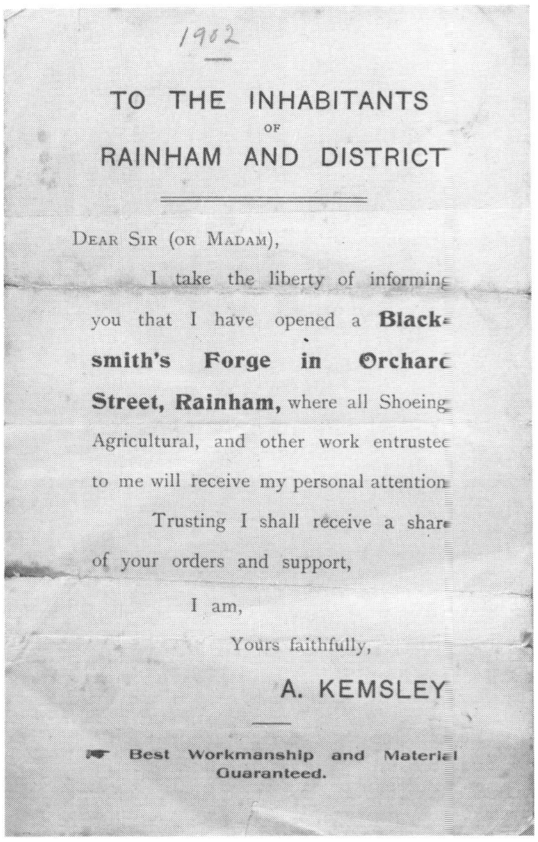
1902

TO THE INHABITANTS
OF
RAINHAM AND DISTRICT

DEAR SIR (OR MADAM),

I take the liberty of informing you that I have opened a **Blacksmith's Forge in Orchard Street, Rainham,** where all Shoeing, Agricultural, and other work entrusted to me will receive my personal attention.

Trusting I shall receive a share of your orders and support,

I am,

Yours faithfully,

A. KEMSLEY

☛ Best Workmanship and Material Guaranteed.

THE FORGE, ORCHARD STREET

In 1902 Mr A. Kemsley who worked as a blacksmith at the forge in Rainham High Street decided to set up his own business in the newly opened up Orchard Street. He built the forge and workshops and, after serving an apprenticeship in Sittingbourne, his son joined him in the business as a wheelwright. During the first world war soldiers were frequent visitors to the forge not only to have their mules shod but also to learn the art of 'cold shoeing' as this would be very necessary in the trenches. Mr A. Kemsley died in 1918 and his son then continued the business employing two blacksmiths to cope with the amount of work available. This of course included repairs of all kinds and the new skill of coachbuilding motor vehicles. Mr Kemsley died in 1950 and the forge was then run for approximately the next 20 years by Reg Young who may be seen in the photograph shaping a horseshoe on the anvil. The forge closed in 1970 and the buildings are now used by two businesses.

Berengrave Lane c.1900

Woodside

High Street, Rainham

BIG CHANGES

The most obvious difference from today to the roads in these pictures is the almost complete absence of traffic and of course the lack of building. The picture of Holding Street gives a slight insight into things to come with two parked cars. It was taken soon after the road was completed in 1929. Today it would be difficult to take any of these views without either cars parked on each side of the road or a continuous stream of passing traffic. Maidstone Road, previously called Bredhurst Lane, has been developed in conjunction with the side roads leading from it. Thus the oldest building is nearest to the A2 and the houses are progressively younger as you journey up to Wigmore Road. Once that process was complete infilling began and more houses appeared — until now very few gaps are left.

Station Road

Holding Street

Maidstone Road (near Kenilworth Drive)

In the centre of this photograph directly beneath the Church Tower may be seen the Royal Cinema. This was one of the smallest cinemas in Kent when it closed in April 1966. A newspaper report at the time said: "It will be sadly missed by courting couples, who were as much attracted by the double seats as by the remarkably cheap prices." The building was then converted into a supermarket by its new owners Vye and Sons who were moving their business from lower down the High Street. Hidsons then redeveloped the old Vye's site and next door Belmont House into their present modern car sales room. (See page 19 for earlier history of the Royal Cinema, previously a Public Hall.)

Numbers 112 and 114 High Street (on the left in this picture) comprised one of the oldest buildings in Rainham, having reputedly been built by the monks of Leeds Abbey to live in whilst they reordered the Church. Certainly it had some very fine old beams particularly the fluted crown post in the attic which was as hard as iron. The building, as so many old places are, was full of nooks and crannies and nothing about the construction appeared to make sense — as it had been lived in and altered over the centuries. After being allowed to deteriorate still further by remaining unoccupied for several years the building was finally declared unsafe in 1984 and demolished (see lower pictures). Belmont House next door as mentioned in the previous caption was demolished some years earlier.

Rainham High Street looking west from near the Kent Reliance Office. At this time the road was called London Road as the High Street began at the White Horse and the Cricketers and ran east as far as Mierscourt Road, at that time called Chapel Lane. From that point eastwards the A2 was known as Broad Walk.

This imposing building was built in 1926 as the gas showrooms with a flat for the manager above. The spacious interior had a large display of all the most modern gas appliances for 1932. The gas board vacated the premises in 1979 when they moved into the centre of Rainham and the building was greatly enlarged to become Manor Farm Restaurant. Durell's Garage could not compete with the larger petrol stations selling at great discounts during the 1970s and continued as a repair garage only until it was finally sold to become a secondhand car sales area.

This view of Rainham in the 1920s has totally changed and is unrecognisable except by people who lived in Rainham at the time. The picture is taken from about the position of Quinnell Street junction with the A2 looking west to Maidstone Road where Manor Farm Restaurant now stands.

Rainham High Street c.1977. The old Builders Merchants shop used by Wards was intended to be preserved as the warden's house when the new Marlborough House sheltered accommodation was built. However it was found to be in such a sad state of disrepair that eventually it became necessary to demolish this building and replace it with a modern construction. This was done in as near the original style as possible and the replacement house does indeed appear very similar – without some of the sagging in the roof perhaps!

The Rainham Fire Brigade was formed in 1901 and by 1908 was quoted as being "an efficient and up to date organization with headquarters situated on the Recreation Ground, the Fire Station housing a modern 22 man manual fire engine and all other appliances for fire fighting." The horses to pull the engine were stabled at the White Horse so it was quite a sight to see when the maroon called out the brigade. Later the fire station moved to this building in Webster Road but has now moved again to a new station built as a part of Signal Court near the Railway Station.

These photographs of the Windmill and Mill House at Otterham were taken in about 1900. The mill stood high on the hill overlooking the creek and one hot day in 1910 it mysteriously caught fire. Despite the efforts of the local volunteer fire brigade from Rainham and men who rushed up from the barges on the river when they saw the fire the total absence of any water meant there was little they could do to prevent it burning to the ground.

Attempts to save some vans and carts from under the mill were hampered by a sow and a big boar who had a family of piglets nearby. Mr Wakeley, the owner, thanked all the men who helped and agreed to pay five shillings compensation to a young barge mate who had badly torn his clothing in the rush to the burning mill.

UPCHURCH POTTERY

During Roman times the largest pottery in the country was along the riverside at Otterham Creek and at similar places where the river was less intrusive on the marshes. A plentiful supply of clay and facilities for both road and sea transport fostered the industry and the blue black pots seen in most museums were probably made here. Discarded pots are still to be found by probing in the mud at low tide.

At the beginning of this century Upchurch Pottery was being made in Seymour Road on the boundary between Upchurch and Rainham. The head potter was Mr Baker and his pots were much sought after for their beautiful coloured glazing. Many people in Rainham still treasure their Upchurch pots. The industry was revived after the Second World War under the title Rainham Pottery in a house near to the Men of Kent. The ware was sold in the Tudor Showroom and Tea Shop (pictured) but sadly the industry created so long ago by the Romans is no more.

MACKLANDS

Macklands House near the bottom of Station Road as it looked from the air in 1960, surrounded by orchards. The farm land was sold for building at the end of that decade and the house itself has since been converted into flats with a collection of bungalows around the grounds. This has been accomplished as sympathetically as possible with many of the large trees remaining together with a good part of the magnificent lawn.

The two photographs below are of the house today.

The old footbridge across the railway line at Rainham Station. When this was built it amazed residents as it appeared overnight so as not to cause interference with the train service. It was demolished just as swiftly in December 1985 but, as the next picture testifies, it was many months before the new bridge slowly grew in its place.

Rainham and Wigmore Community Centre near Rainham Station just before the old cottages were demolished. This was partly to provide better access but also the sale of the land for building provided much needed funds to enable the conversion to a Community Centre to go ahead.

SNOW SCENES

As this book was being prepared at the beginning of 1987 Kent suffered one of its worst blizzards in living memory. For a few days Rainham became a village again, almost completely cut off from the rest of the world. To record this period of January 1987 when time stood still I decided to include a page of pictures to remind us in future years of the time schools closed for up to a fortnight because of snow!

1

2

3

6

7

4

5

8

1. St Margaret's Church from the back of the Cricketers.
2. Doug Smith (caretaker) clears the icicles from St Margaret's Nursery School building.
3. High Street traffic lights.
4. Queue for milk, Rainham High Street.
5. A van not going anywhere.
6. This train made it – slowly.
7. Orchard Street.
8. The old parsonage at night.